DOC

TRASH
TALK

THE SEVEN ROBOTS

Raintree is an imprint of Capstone
Global Library Limited, a company
incorporated in England and Wales
having its registered office at 7
Pilgrim Street, London, EC4V 6LB –
Registered company number: 6695582

www.raintree.co.uk
myorders@raintree.co.uk

Text © Capstone Global Library
Limited 2016

Designed by Hilary Wacholz
Edited by Sean Tulien
Original illustrations © Capstone 2016
Illustrated by Jimena Sanchez

ISBN 978 1 4747 1027 5 (paperback)
20 19 18 17 16
10 9 8 7 6 5 4 3 2 1

British Library Cataloguing in Publication
Data: a full catalogue record for
this book is available from the British

FAR OUT
FAIRY TALES

INTRODUCING...

QUEEN REGENT

SNOW WHITE

FAR OUT FAIRY TALES

SNOW WHITE
AND THE
SEVEN ROBOTS

A GRAPHIC NOVEL

BY LOUISE SIMONSON
ILLUSTRATED BY JIMENA SÁNCHEZ

Every morning, the Queen Regent spoke to the satellite that monitored their planet...

Secret eye above the sky, who is the smartest that you spy?

And every morning, the satellite showed the Queen Regent her own face.

I watch your world. I can't deny. The queen's the smartest one I spy.

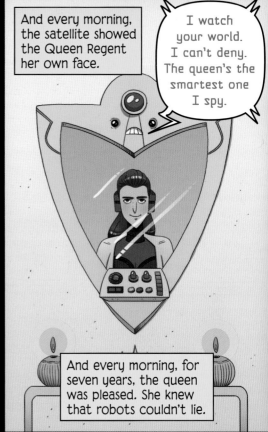

And every morning, for seven years, the queen was pleased. She knew that robots couldn't lie.

Until...

What is *this*, Snow?

A robot kitten! I made it for your birthday!

All by yourself? That is *remarkable!*

That same morning, when the queen asked her question, the satellite had a different answer.

I watch your world. I cannot lie. Snow White will be the smartest, by and by.

No! She will steal my crown! The child must go!

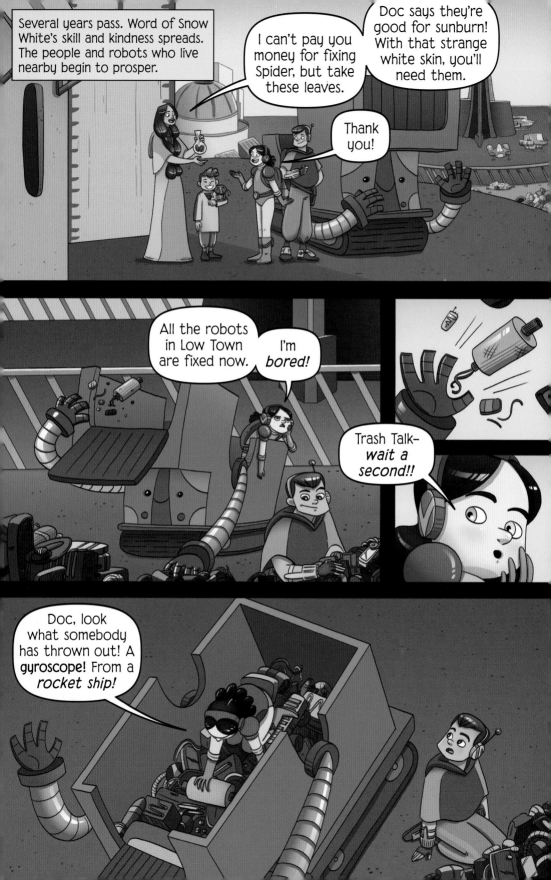

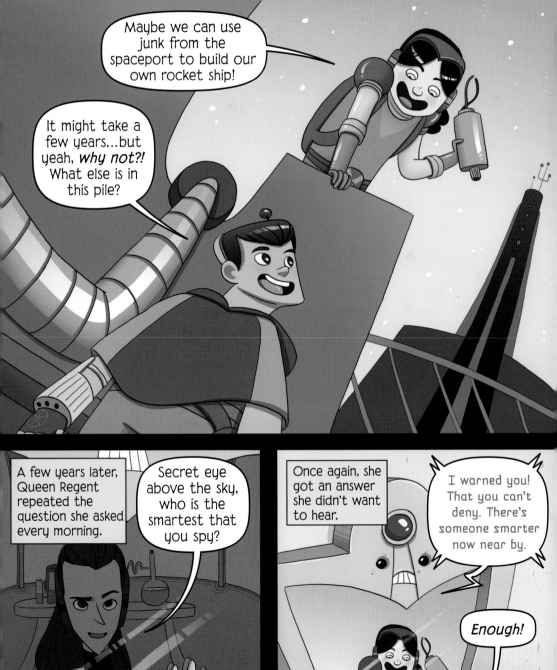

Maybe we can use junk from the spaceport to build our own rocket ship!

It might take a few years...but yeah, *why not?!* What else is in this pile?

A few years later, Queen Regent repeated the question she asked every morning.

Secret eye above the sky, who is the smartest that you spy?

Once again, she got an answer she didn't want to hear.

I warned you! That you can't deny. There's someone smarter now near by.

Enough!

Get me that Rubbish Robot! I want him here— *immediately!*

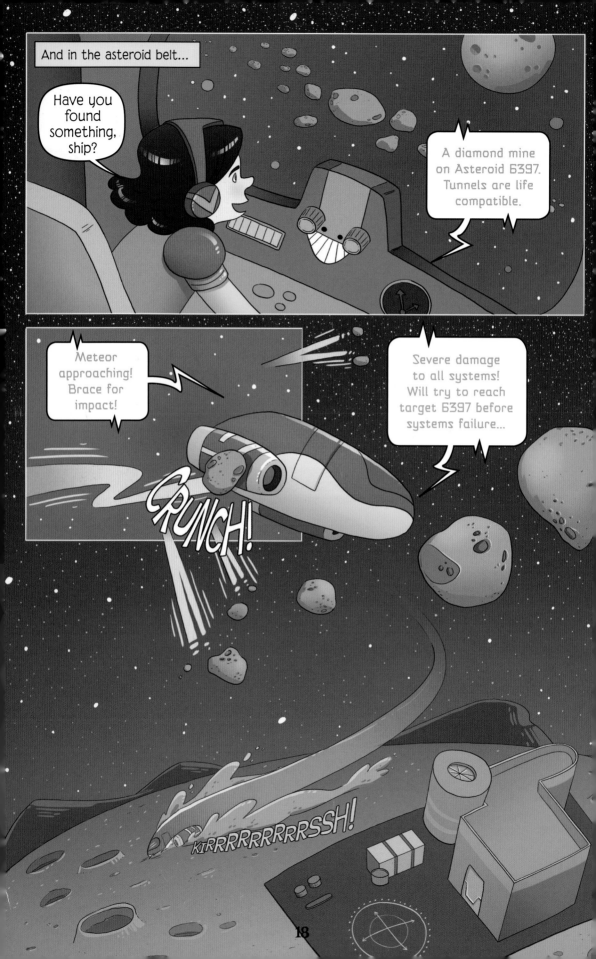

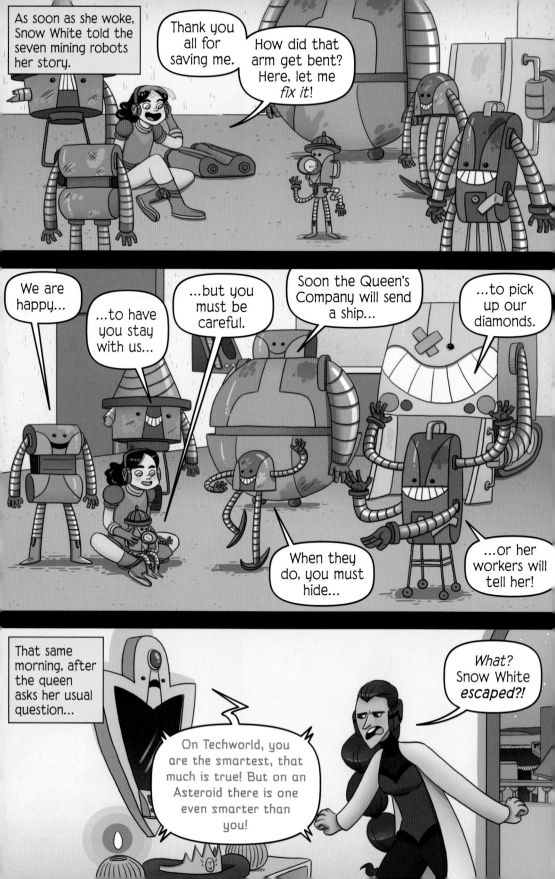

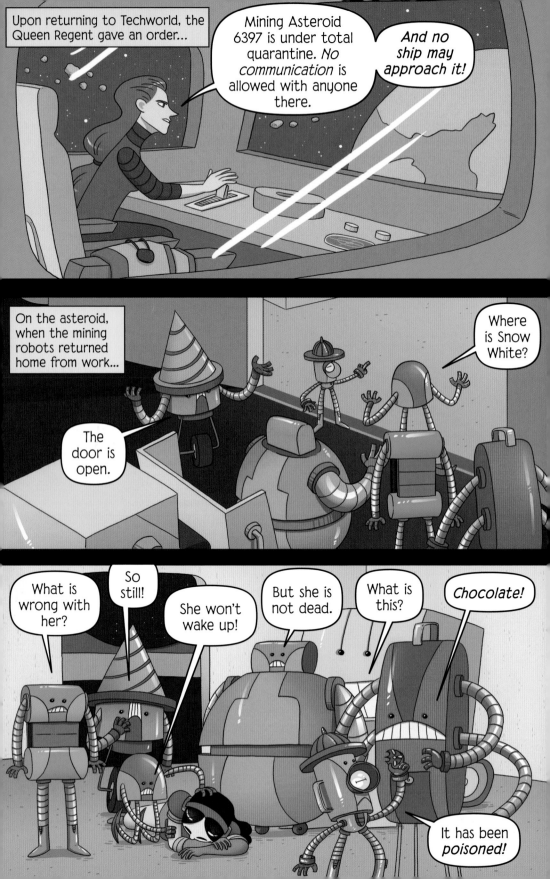

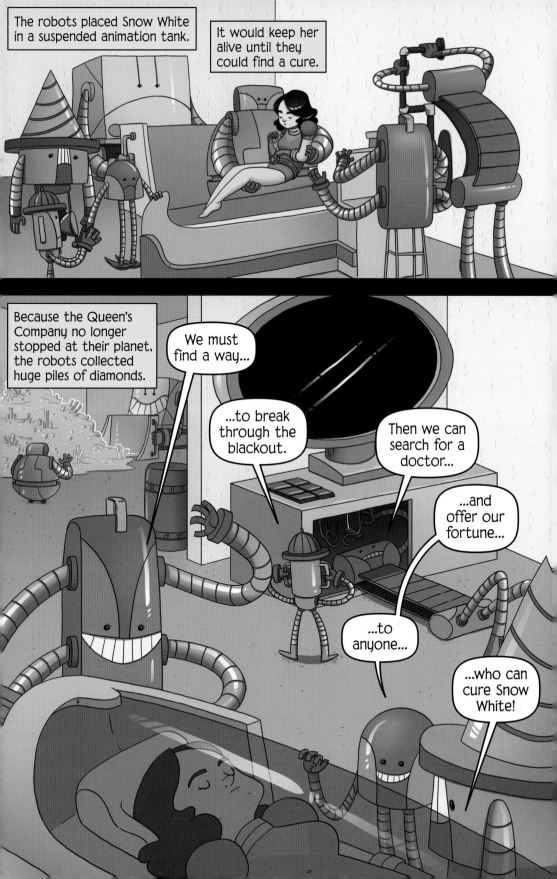

ALL ABOUT THE ORIGINAL TALE!

The story of Snow White was first published by the Brothers Grimm in 1812. This fairy tale tells the story of a queen who wishes for a daughter with skin as white as snow, lips as red as blood and jet-black hair. She gets her wish, but tragically dies during childbirth.

Snow White's father then marries a beautiful but selfish woman. Every day, the new queen asks a magic mirror who the most beautiful woman alive is. And every day, the mirror says it's the queen—until one day the mirror names Snow White instead.

The queen decides to have Snow killed. She orders a huntsman to murder her, but he can't make himself do the deed so he abandons her in the forest instead. Snow comes across a tiny cottage with seven small beds. As it turns out, seven dwarves live there, and they let her stay with them in exchange for keeping their home tidy and making their meals.

Soon after, the magic mirror tells the queen where Snow is hiding. The queen arrives disguised as a farmer's wife and offers Snow a poisoned apple, which puts Snow into a permanent state of sleep. When the dwarves return from work, they think Snow is dead, so they place her in a glass coffin.

One day, a prince comes along and is struck by Snow White's beauty. The dwarves let the prince take the coffin, presumably so she can have a proper burial. As the dwarves carry the coffin away, they trip and drop it. The bump dislodges the chunk of apple that was caught in Snow's throat, and she awakens! (In some versions of the tale, it's the prince's kiss that wakes Snow White from her endless sleep.) Either way, Snow falls in love with the prince at first sight. They marry, live happily ever after, and the evil queen is punished for her misdeeds.

In this far out version of the fairy tale, it's Snow White's inner beauty and intelligence that the queen fears. Check out this book's other twists to the timeless tale...

A FAR OUT GUIDE TO SNOW WHITE'S TALE TWISTS!

The all-knowing magic mirror is replaced by an all-seeing space satellite!

Dwarves helped the original Snow White. In this tale, robots come to her aid!

Instead of a poisoned apple putting Snow to sleep, poisoned chocolate is the culprit.

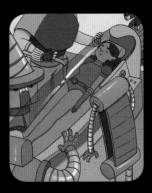

This cryo-tank preserves Snow White instead of the glass coffin in the original tale.

1

Why does Doc throw Snow White's rucksack into the mud? How do you know?

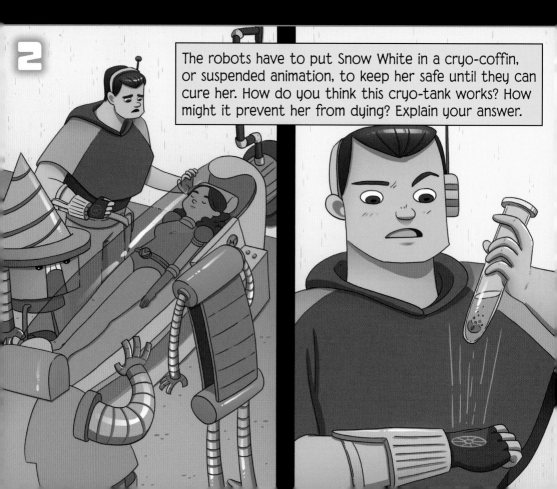

2

The robots have to put Snow White in a cryo-coffin, or suspended animation, to keep her safe until they can cure her. How do you think this cryo-tank works? How might it prevent her from dying? Explain your answer.

3

KISS.

What do you think caused Snow White to wake up? Why?

4

A moral is a lesson that a story teaches. What do you think the moral of this story is? Why?

5

What big role did this little robot play in the story? How did he end up saving Snow White? Why do you think he helped?

AUTHOR

Louise Simonson writes about monsters, science fiction and fantasy characters, and superheroes. She wrote the award-winning Power Pack series, several best-selling X-Men titles, Web of Spider-man for Marvel Comics and Superman: Man of Steel and Steel for DC Comics. She has also written many books for kids. She is married to comic artist and writer Walter Simonson and lives in the suburbs of New York City, USA.

ILLUSTRATOR

Jimena Sánchez was born in Mexico City, Mexico, in 1980. She studied illustration in the Escuela Nacional de Artes Plásticas (National School of Arts) and has since worked and lived in the United States as well as Spain. Jimena now lives in Mexico City again, working as an illustrator and comic book artist. Her art has appeared in many children's books and magazines.

GLOSSARY

align   arrange things so that they form a line or are in proper position

apprentice   person who learns a job or skill by working for a fixed period of time for someone who is good at that job or skill

aptitude   natural ability to do something or to learn something

brace   prepare for something difficult or unpleasant

cure   something (such as a drug or medical treatment) that stops a disease and makes someone healthy again

formula   list of the ingredients used for making something (such as a medicine or a drink)

integrity   quality of being honest and fair

malfunctioned   broken or failed to work properly

possess   have or own something

prospector   someone who searches the land for special or valuable minerals, rocks, gems, etc.

prosper   become very successful usually by making a lot of money

quarantine   situation of being kept away from others to prevent a disease from spreading

regent   person who rules a kingdom when the king or queen is not able to rule

stead   in place of something or someone

vain   too proud of yourself

AWESOMELY EVER after.

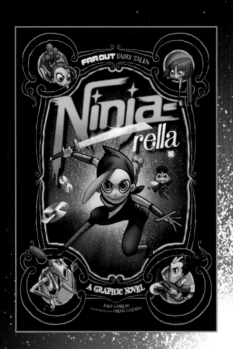

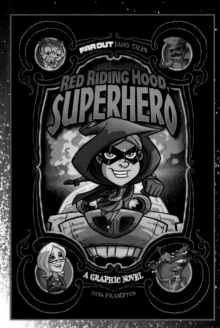

FAR OUT FAIRY TALES